Government Services

by Ann-Marie Kishel

first step nonfiction

Lerner Publications Company · Minneapolis

Our **government** takes care
of us in many ways.

Government **services** help meet our needs.

Some services make our communities better.

Garbage collectors take our trash away.

The postal service delivers
our mail.

We can send letters
anywhere in the world.

The park service **protects** our parks.

We play in parks.

Some services help us learn.

We learn at school and at the library.

Some services protect us.

Police officers and firefighters keep us safe.

A receipt dated within 90 days is required for ALL returns & exchanges. Giving a gift? Include a gift receipt!

```
237000013      4X6 DIGITAL        T      5.00
               25 @ 0.20


T = MN TAX  7.0000% on   SUBTOTAL      5.00
                            5.00       0.35
                           TOTAL       5.35

                  CASH PAYMENT        20.00
                   CHANGE DUE         14.65


   RECEIPT ID# 2-6254-1375-0069-1198-8
                       TM#****8151
        VCD# 758-289-354

            Save ALL Receipts
   Give Gift Receipts & GiftCards
      Ask about Receipt Lookup
```

Taxes help pay for these services.

Taxes are money we pay to the government.

There are services all around us.

What services do you use?

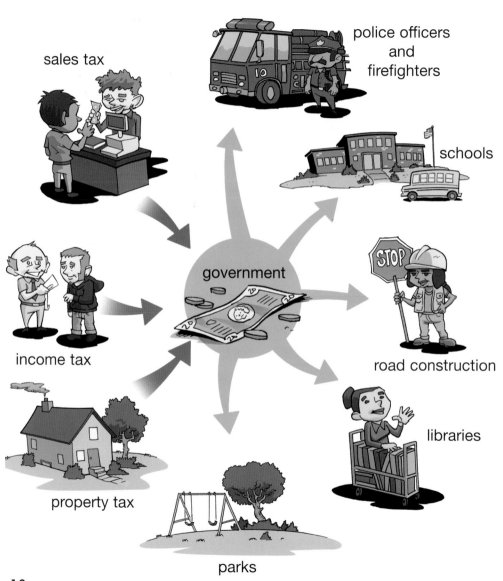

sales tax

police officers
and
firefighters

schools

government

income tax

road construction

property tax

libraries

parks

18

Taxes and Services

The U.S. government provides us with many services. Who pays for these services? We do. People living in the United States pay taxes. A tax is money we pay to the government. We pay tax on things we buy at the store. The government takes taxes from people's paychecks. Adults also pay tax on their houses. The government uses the money from taxes to pay for the services we use.

Government Services Facts

 The Treasury Department deals with money matters. Its U.S. Mint makes all the coins, and its Bureau of Engraving and Printing makes all the paper money.

 The Department of Transportation makes sure people and goods can travel safely and quickly around the United States.

The Environmental Protection Agency (EPA) works to protect people and our planet.

 The Library of Congress is the national library for the United States.

 The Smithsonian Institution runs many museums and the National Zoo.

 The National Aeronautics and Space Administration (NASA) explores space.

Glossary

 government – the group of people who run a country

 protects – keeps someone or something safe

 services – work, help, or aid that government offers

 taxes – money paid for government services

Index

The photographs in this book are reproduced with the permission of: © William Thomas Cain/Getty Images, front cover; © Tannen Maury/Stringer/AFP/Getty Images, pp. 2, 22 (top); © Comstock Royalty Free, pp. 3, 11; © age fotostock/SuperStock, pp. 4, 22 (second from bottom); © Valerie Huselid/Independent Picture Service, p. 5; © Henry Diltx/CORBIS, p. 6; © PhotoDisc Royalty Free by Getty Images, p. 7; © Tom Bean, p. 8; © Royalty-Free/CORBIS, p. 9; © Digital Vision by Getty Images, p. 10, © Anton Vengo/SuperStock, pp. 12, 22 (second from top); © Brooks Kraft/CORBIS, p. 13; © Todd Strand/Independent Picture Service, pp. 14, 22 (bottom); © Brie Cohen/Independent Picture Service, p. 15; AP/Wide World Photos, p. 16; © Eyewire by Getty Images, p. 17.

Diagram on p. 18 by Bill Hauser/Independent Picture Service.

Lerner Publications Company,
a division of Lerner Publishing Group
241 First Avenue North
Minneapolis, MN 55401 U.S.A.

Website address: www.lernerbooks.com

Library of Congress Cataloging-in-Publication Data

Kishel, Ann-Marie.
        Government services / by Ann-Marie Kishel.
            p.   cm. — (First step nonfiction)
        Includes index.
        ISBN-13: 978-0-8225-6397-6 (lib. bdg. : alk. paper)
        ISBN-10: 0-8225-6397-5 (lib. bdg. : alk. paper)
        1. Public administration—United States—Juvenile literature. 2. Administrative agencies—United States—Juvenile literature. 3. Civil service—United States—Juvenile literature. I. Title.
    JK421.K55 2007
    351.73—dc22   2006018629